Getting to  in

Fund Raising

Getting to Yes in FUND RAISING

by Betty Stallings

Getting to Yes in Fund Raising

copyright © 1991 by Betty Stallings

Published by **Heritage Arts**
1807 Prairie Avenue
Downers Grove, IL 60515
(708) 964-1194
FAX (708) 964-0841

ISBN 0-911029-33-8

ALL RIGHTS RESERVED—No portion of this book may be reproduced in any form without express written permission of the author.

PRINTED IN THE UNITED STATES OF AMERICA

With Appreciation

- to my teachers, mentors, and funders who gave me the tools and courage to bring visions into reality, through fund raising

- to **Sue Vineyard** for nudging me to finally get this book written and for her support and counsel along the way

- to **Helen Robinson**, a dear friend, former colleague and marvelous editor who patiently read and re-read the manuscript looking for yet one more missing comma

- to friends, **Cindy Leung** and **Jane Vincent,** who loaned their artistic advice and touch to the book

- to my husband, **Charles**, who has patiently guided me through my trials of writing my first book, via computer and

- to my daughter, **Debbie**, who has always known how to get to **Yes!** Through her energetic spirit and determination, I have learned much about the art of persuasion.

Dedication

to my mother and father,

Ruth and Brooke Bright,

who through the examples of their lives,

taught me to care for others, and to

persist with my dreams

and to **Sharon**,

my youngest daughter,

to whom I have always promised to

dedicate my first book,

I do so with love!

Getting to Yes in Fund Raising

Table of Contents

Introduction xi

Chapter 1 - Philosophical Mind-set in
             Fund Raising 1
             Breaking Down Stereotypes 2
             No Charity, Please 3
             Marketing Concept 4
             Partnerships 5
             Nonprofit Businesses 7
             Visualize Success 8
             Supporters Give to Winners 9
             Passionate Belief in What You Do 11

Chapter 2 - Problem Statement 15
             Narrowing the Definition
                of the Problem 16
             Connecting Your Organization's
                Background With The Problem 17
             Demonstrating Evidence to Support the Need 18
             Determining Collaboration Potential 19

Chapter 3 - Program Idea and Program
             Objectives 21
             Your Plan to Solve the Problem 22
             What You Hope to Accomplish 23
             Program Evaluation 25

Chapter 4 -	**Planning and Preparation** **29**	
	The Budget 30	
	Timing Issues 31	
	Future Funding..32	
	Tips for Putting Together an Agency Prospectus 33	
	Tips in Researching Appropriate Funders........................34	
	Types of Foundation and Corporate Giving Structures 36	
Chapter 5 -	**Preliminary Interest of Funder** **41**	
	Phone Contact 42	
	Letter of Intent 46	
	Pre-proposal Interview 47	
Chapter 6 -	**Proposal Preparation** **51**	
	Making Your Proposal Stand Out 51	
	Writing a Good Introduction and Proposal Summary....................53	
	Clear, Concise and Alive Writing 54	
	Be Aware of Jargon 54	
	Proposal Critique by Outsider 55	
	Credibility Information in the Appendix 55	
	Connecting to Funder's Interest 56	
	Cover Letter 57	
Chapter 7 -	**Patience and Persistence** **59**	
	Did The Proposal Arrive? 59	
	Sending Updates to the Funder 60	
	Asking for "the Status of My Proposal" 60	
	Handling a Rejection Letter.....................61	
	Thanking Funder for Their Consideration 63	

Chapter 8 -	**Persuasive Presentations To Funding Sources** 65	

- Establishing a Personal Link with the Funder 66
- Dress Like People You Are Going to See 67
- Where to Hold the Meeting 68
- Be Prepared and Professional 68
- Advance Information on the Meeting 69
- Use of Volunteers to Present Your Case 70
- Variety in Presentation 71
- Influence of Voice Inflection/Body Language 72
- Knowing Where You Stand After the Meeting 72

Chapter 9 -	**Patience and Persistence (Again!)** 75	

- If You are Turned Down 76
- The Magic Question to Ask 77

Chapter 10 -	**Presentation of the Check** 79	

- Celebrate the News! 80

Chapter 11 -	**Proliferation of Thank Yous and Perpetuation of the Contact** 81	

- Key Characteristics of Recognition 81
- 3 Rules for Recognizing Donors 82
- The Power in Recognition 87
- Perpetuation of the Contact 89

Chapter 12 -	**Process Evaluation** 91	

- 8 Key Evaluation Questions 91
- PIE Method of Evaluation 96

Personal Tidbits 97
Parting Comments 99
Appendix 101
Bibliography 104
About the Author 105

Introduction

There are literally thousands of organizations doing worthy, noble activities in response to a myriad of community needs. Why is it when seeking funds, some of these organizations get to **yes** while others get the "Sorry we can't help you, but keep up the good work" letter?

Sixteen years ago when I naively started to raise funds to establish a volunteer center, I thought that the best programs would receive the funding. When that bubble burst, I thought that writing the best proposal or having the most persuasive "dog and pony show" would do it. But, alas, I learned the hard way. I heard, "No, but good luck," more often than I would like to remember. Fortunately, I have been blessed with persistence, or very early in the effort I would have dropped my dream and all hopes of funding it. I had to continually remind myself that Babe Ruth struck out 1,130 times in his career.

Persistence, knowledge and experience eventually paid off and at the end of my fundraising efforts with the volunteer center, we had the ultimate "high" in fund raising. We sent a $76,000 proposal to 3 potential funders and all three said, **Yes!**

Many folks who followed the successful growth of the volunteer center thought that we had been given a magic pen and asked for the secrets of our success. In response, I began to develop and present a number of workshops on fund raising and partnerships.

With the encouragement of many workshop participants, I have written this book to share these tips with:

- people who are beginning to seek corporate or foundation funds for their nonprofit organization or volunteer program,
- organizations who are hearing "No" and are wondering why, or
- seasoned fund raisers looking for some inspiration or, perhaps, one new idea to increase their chances of getting to **Yes.**

This is not an in-depth, how-to book, but rather a compilation of many practical tips (and secrets) I wish I had known when I started fund raising for a cause I cared about passionately.

Although the focus is on fund raising in the foundation and corporation world, you will find that most of the tips and principles are applicable when approaching any individual or organization for funding.

The contents for this book were primarily drawn from the wise words of many mentors, authors and workshop leaders who gave me the courage and the tools to try fund raising. It also reflects my 16 years experience in fund raising for nonprofit organizations and the contributions of many funders who willingly shared tips with me in answer to my quest, "What are the *real reasons* that funding requests are successful in **Getting to YES** ?"

Philosophical Mind-set In Fund Raising

Essential to success in fund raising are the attitudes and philosophy we take with us as we search for support. No experience made this more clear to me than one meeting I observed recently at a state conference on volunteering.

When I entered the room, my attention was drawn to two flip charts, one of which read, "The Haves" and the other, "The Have Nots." The speaker was referring to nonprofit organizations as "The Have Nots" and corporations as "The Haves." Light bulbs went on in my head. This attitude, I thought, is the very reason many nonprofit organizations are not successful at fund raising. They see themselves as lowly beggars at the whim of the rich and powerful. As long as we hold these and other demeaning thoughts, we simply cannot feel good about fund raising. As a result, we will be far less successful in our endeavors.

There are eight significant factors which I feel make up a healthy mind-set towards fund raising.

☐

Breaking Down Stereotypes

When I am training with an audience which includes both profit and nonprofit folks, I frequently lead them through the following exercise.[1]

I ask the nonprofit participants to close their eyes and envision a stereotypical person from the corporate world. You don't need a big imagination to guess what we discover. Corporate types are described as numbers oriented, male, well dressed, cold, trendy, Republicans, stone-hearted, bottom-line focused, etc. At this point the corporate folks in the room are squirming uncomfortably, so I turn to them and give them a similar opportunity to describe their nonprofit counterparts. We are described as poor managers, emotional, no financial sense, female, neurotic bleeding hearts, Democrats, etc.

After the nervous laughter calms down, people begin to refute their stereotypes. (It is always wonderful to have in the workshop a female corporate person who is dressed very casually, a Democrat and lacking in accounting skills. I can't tell you how often that happens.)

The obvious point is how often we stereotype people, particularly when we

Philosophical Mind-set In Fund Raising

enter a culture different from our own. As long as we hold stereotypes, we will find internal barriers which hinder the development of a productive relationship.

When we reach out and ask support from another person, we must be open to each other as individuals.

☐

No Charity, Please

When one hears the word charity, it connotes a sense of the poor and the needy. In many cases our organizations assist low-income individuals or people with great needs. When, however, our organizations are looking for support in fulfilling our mission, we must see ourselves, (as Kim Klein, noted fund raiser, says,) **"as applicants, not a supplicants."**[2] As supplicants, we put ourselves in a lower position, just grateful for any crumb thrown in our direction.

Feel the difference when you say to a potential donor, "I have come to you with an opportunity to assist in the solution of a community problem." In essence, you are not begging, you are offering an investment in their community. When I am feeling very positive about a proposal, I frequently say, "I would like to offer you the first opportunity to be a partner with us in the solution of this problem." That approach is particularly successful when there is healthy competition between banks or other businesses in your community.

Getting To Yes In Fund Raising

In my experience, people who operate out of the begging mode often suffer from burn out. They may leave our organizations with feelings of resentment regarding donor attitudes and responses.

On the other hand, individuals who walk into a potential funder with their heads high, sincerely offering an investment opportunity, frequently receive an eager, "Yes, we'd love to participate."

☐

Marketing Concept

The transition from begging to marketing represents a profound change in fund raising and volunteer recruitment. People or funding bodies do not want to simply be "giving away" their money. They want to know what value(s) they will receive in return for their gift. At the heart of marketing is an understanding of this exchange of values. Nonprofit organizations are almost always initiating this exchange. Too often we only plead our case in hopes that someone out there will hear our plea and want to help. This one-way form of fund raising can take a long time, in some situations, forever.

Before asking for support, it is always important to ask the questions, "Why would this individual, or funder, want to support us? What is the exchange for them in this transaction?"

Marketing was involved when our volunteer center was accepted as a United Way organization. The competition was extremely heavy. Four organizations out

Philosophical Mind-set In Fund Raising

of 144 were to be accepted. Knowing that all organizations applying were excellent ones responding to critical human needs in the San Francisco Bay Area, we decided to explore the question, "What would be in it for United Way to include our organization in its family of agencies?"

The answer was clear. Our community had recently begun a transformation from a bedroom community to a relocation area for inner city corporations. Since United Way is primarily a fund raising organization, these corporations could prove to be a great support to their fund drive. With these thoughts in mind, we developed our marketing strategy. We emphasized that United Way needed our organization as a strong visible United Way agency in this community, particularly since there were no United Way agencies in our valley. We were one of the four agencies selected that year.

The important thing to remember: we were not necessarily the most worthy, noble or successful organization applying. We were a good organization that understood and used the marketing concept in our proposal. I am convinced that this was what got us to **"Yes, and welcome to the United Way family."**

☐

Partnerships

Another critical aspect of the fund raising mind-set is having an orientation toward the partnership concept. Think how difficult it is to create a partnership

5

Getting To Yes In Fund Raising

if both parties are not seen as giving and gaining from the collaboration. Too often in our desperation to get funding, our thinking is shortsighted. Rather than looking at the funder as an ongoing partner and ourselves as a significant contributor to that partnership, we run in for a quick fix. (The "Help, we're desperate!" pitch.) We lose many opportunities to establish long term relationships.

When I looked back over my 13 years at the Valley Volunteer Center, it became clear that our fund raising success was closely tied to our partnerships with corporations, businesses and foundations in our area (Macy's, The Hilton, AT&T, Clorox, The San Francisco Foundation and numerous others).

We often hear from corporate or foundation funders, "We can only help you once and then you must find other sources." I discovered, however, that if we involved them as partners in the solution of a community problem which was of interest to them, they frequently wanted to continue working with us. Additionally, when the collaboration was positive and successful, we even experienced the ultimate high in fund raising. A current funder came to us and said, "Can we continue to be part of your program? How can we help?" It is always such a wonderful experience to be the one in the position to say **Yes!**

Philosophical Mind-set In Fund Raising

Nonprofit Businesses

Organizations which are particularly successful in getting to **yes** with corporations are ones that use excellent business principles in managing their organizations. These organizations have sound financial recordkeeping systems, frequently produce an annual report and can make articulate, concise oral and written presentations. They are also able to demonstrate that their organization goes through annual strategic planning and evaluation. The one complaint I have heard most often from business and foundation funders is their concern for the loose, or nonexistent, business practices of nonprofit organizations seeking support from them.

It was helpful for me when first seeking funds to begin to think of my organization as a human service business. We sought help from key business leaders in the community by bringing them onto our board. Business board members can be tremendously helpful in opening doors for you into their world.

Small businesses that run on less stringent business practices may be considerably more lenient with small nonprofits seeking support from them. So, until you are comfortable that your organization is operating on excellent business principles, you may wish to concentrate more on small, local businesses. Here the gift is usually dependent on personally knowing the owner, rather than on your business or presentation skills.

I would hope that as we in the non-profit world become more sophisticated in business and management principles, the corporate world will begin to think of us as businesses providing human service or educational work. Too often we are still seen as charity workers, or worse yet, do-gooders. Unfortunately, we have a ways to go to alter our stereotypical image.

☐

Visualize Success

One of the most powerful exercises we have at our finger tips is visualization. I have always been fascinated by the mental exercise that superb athletes go through before attempting their physical feats. They see themselves going over the vault, hitting a home run, staying on the balance beam. I discovered how effective this exercise could be before writing a solicitation letter or giving a presentation to a funder. As our organization began to develop or enhance a new program, we would visualize it as something already accomplished. We imagined what it looked like, how many people were touched by it, the impact it was having in our community.

What we discovered in using visualization was that our energy and optimism were maximized. We truly believed that it was not a case of "if" our grant would be funded, but "when." Approaching funders with this genuinely positive feeling creates a significant impact on potential supporters.

When I write letters to potential funders I frequently think of a tip that

Philosophical Mind-set In Fund Raising

Kim Klein gave in one of her workshops. She indicated that when you are writing a letter requesting funding, it is very important to visualize them shaking their heads and saying, **Yes!** The letter might start out by saying, "We are aware of your interest in the homeless of our city and are aware of your former generous response to their needs." (Reader shakes head, **Yes!**) The letter ends by saying, "And therefore, we know that you will want to consider supporting this important effort to provide clothing and housing to the disadvantaged of our city." (Reader, hopefully, shakes head,**Yes!**)

You may want to look back at some of your unsuccessful solicitation letters and see how you could apply this principle to make your appeal more likely to get to **Yes.**

☐

Supporters Give to Winners

Another important factor in the philosophical mind-set for fund raising is our awareness that supporters want to give to winners - needy winners, perhaps, but winners, nonetheless. Initially I did not want our organization to look too good for fear that we wouldn't appear to need support. And so I went to extreme efforts to "look poor".

Looking poor to some unsophisticated, small donors is sometimes successful. What we learned, however, was that most often, major givers, whether they be individuals, corporations or foundations,

Getting To Yes In Fund Raising

Graphics Donated by:

were looking to invest their money in a solid, first class organization that appeared to have a good future and significant respect in the community.

In our organization, the dilemma of not wishing to look too wealthy, but desirous of looking professional, was solved by one of our corporate partners. AT&T agreed to do much of our graphic art work. We were able to give them credit for our "look" by acknowledging them for their graphic art and printing contributions on our brochures, flyers, etc. And our funders knew that we had not spent donor dollars for upgraded P.R. materials.

What many funders have told me over and over again is that they are not interested in merely **extending the demise of an organization**, but rather wish to become a partner with a successful, visible organization doing significant work in their community. Many organizations with whom I have consulted have held the mind-set of simply looking for funders to keep the organization or programs going. Their requests to funders had often met with the "Sorry, but good luck" letter. Just a change in approach to the funders frequently turned a no into an enthusiastic **yes**. Frequently the yes came for the same program request that was formerly denied.

Again, we learn that it is infrequently the program that is the cause for the rejection; more often it is our philosophy and approach to the potential supporter.

Philosophical Mind-set In Fund Raising

Passionate Belief in What You Do

I believe that the major reason so many people give up fund raising, is because they do not hold a strong, passionate belief in their organization or program. One executive businessman said it well when he described the preferred qualities of a person seeking funds from his corporation. He said we should strive to be **"low-key, professional missionaries."** Fund raising is tough, competitive work and you must truly be sold on your product. Without this energy, direction and enthusiasm, many folks want to quit after they hear no a few times. When discouraged, it is important to reconnect with the vision of what you are trying to create or accomplish through your fund raising efforts. If you cannot draw energy from this vision, it may be time to look for another cause.

Someone pointed out to me that I should always remember the last four letters of the word, enthusiasm /iasm/ which stands for **I Am Sold M**yself. Without personal commitment to an idea, a product or an organization, how can you ever persuade another person to join with you?

Remember:

When you are selling ideas, you are basically trying to transfer your feelings to another individual so that they will say, **Yes.**

Concluding Exercise

Before going on, I suggest that you and your organization examine the mind-set that you hold about fund raising. Ask yourself these questions:

1. Do you harbor stereotypes of those from whom you seek to develop partnerships or to seek support?
2. Do you see yourself as a "lowly charity" seeking support from the powerful?
3. Do you always examine what benefits your donor will receive from supporting your organization?
4. When you seek support, is it generally for short term assistance or do you think of a potential long term partnership?
5. Is your organization run as a non-profit business?
6. Do you visualize your funder saying yes to your requests and do you practice the mental exercise of exploring how your new or enhanced service is benefiting your clients and community?
7. Does your organization promote itself as a needy charity or as a winner?
8. Do you and members of your organization passionately believe in the mission of your organization and can you/they articulate that mission with the qualities of a "low-key, professional missionary?"

Philosophical Mind-set In Fund Raising

Exploring your responses to these questions may well be the key determinant in the future success of your fund raising efforts.

□

Footnotes:

1. This exercise is one which was shared with me by Mike King, V.P. for Marketing, United Way of Dallas, Texas.
2. Klein, Kim. Grassroots Fundraising Videotapes. The Youth Project, 2335 18th Street N.W., Washington, D.C. 2000.

Problem Statement

This first step in fund raising is the development of a clear problem (case) statement, concisely addressing the need(s) of your clients. To alleviate or solve this problem, you develop a service or program, (A problem may be that your low-income clients are not getting proper medical treatment due to lack of available transportation to medical facilities. Your solution is to purchase a van and provide transportation.)

One of the most flagrant mistakes made in funding requests is that the problem statement is written as a need of the agency, not the clients. (e.g., <u>our agency needs</u> a computer so that we can run a more efficient organization.) What we must realize is that the computer is the solution to a problem that we have in serving the needs of our clients. Therefore, we must begin with the definition of their needs and problems. As Susan Scribner says in her excellent booklet, How To Ask For Money Without Fainting!

"...agencies have no needs. Clients do...Donors don't give US money. They give us money for our CLIENTS."[1]

Pointers in the Development of a Problem Statement

- Narrow the definition of the problem.
- Make a logical connection between your organization's background and the problem.
- Demonstrate evidence to support the need.
- Indicate ways you will be collaborating with other organizations dealing with this problem.

Narrowing the Definition of the Problem

Frequently an organization will paint a broad picture of a problem, never narrowing it down to the specific issues that are solvable by that organization. This may leave a potential funder thinking that all the money in the world could not solve the problem. This example of overkill usually occurs when the applicant feels that it must draw a picture of enormous need to convince the funder to support them. All this generally does is to convince the funder of the unlikelihood

Problem Statement

that this organization could make any significant impact on this problem.

Funders are more apt to say, **Yes** when the problem is narrowed down to something that your organization can hope to accomplish within a limited amount of time and with reasonable additional resources.

☐

Connecting Your Organization's Background with the Problem

Most funders want evidence that your organization has the experience, expertise and reputation of working in the area of your program request. If the problem is newly identified, as was AIDS a decade ago, they will want evidence that your organization has strong leadership and a track record of successful program planning and execution. A few small or special interest foundations support high risk or experimental activities. Most, I found, are very conservative and are most likely to say "**Yes**" when the project or program appears to have a good chance for success. (Remember, funders like to support winners!)

During times of tight money, many organizations begin to "chase dollars", in other words, develop new programs in their organizations in areas which seem to be currently popular with funding sources. I specifically remember a Volunteer Center board retreat when one of my directors asked why we didn't go into day care since so much money seemed available in that area. Fortunately most board members were more closely tuned into

17

our mission and saw the pitfalls to this type of fund raising.

This is not to say, however, that you should ignore the current trends in funding. Many times they can be creatively worked into your funding pattern without altering the mission of your organization or program. An example of this was when our organization began to extend our internship program, originally responding to needs of older re-entry women, into areas of high risk youth, young single women, etc. The needs for these populations were well documented and we had a program that, with small modifications, could be helpful in meeting their needs. Conveniently, United Way and many foundations were focusing on the critical employment issues of these populations. As I viewed it, this was a perfect example of what Zig Ziglar calls, **"opportunity meeting preparation."**[2]

Demonstrating Evidence to Support the Need

There is nothing quite so distressing to a funder as to read a proposal that says, "We don't have a community center in our area, therefore, we need one." The mere fact that there isn't a particular service, program, theater, etc. in your area does not necessarily merit the funds to construct one. You must always be able to support the existence of a problem through evidence of a need. This evidence can come from statistics (not ones gathered around the world, but those in the geo-

Problem Statement

graphic area you are impacting). County and city planning offices are excellent sources for data, interpretations and projections related to the most recent census figures. You may also get advice from groups in your community concerned about the problem, from prospective clients, from other organizations working in your community, and from professionals in the field.

☐

Determining Collaboration Potential

One of the key components that today's sophisticated funders are looking for is how you will be working with organizations in your service area who are dealing with similar problems. Organizations that are leaders in collaborative efforts to solve significant problems will, I firmly believe, be the organizations most likely to get to **Yes** in the nineties and beyond.

☐

Footnotes:

1. Scribner, Susan. <u>How To Ask For Money Without Fainting.</u> (Scribner & Associates) p.6. (This is a great little book on asking individuals for money.)

Program Idea and Program Objectives

Once you have clearly defined your clients' need or problem, it is important that you ask yourself 3 questions involving your proposed solution to that problem.

Key Questions

1. Through what means do I plan to solve this problem? (program/methods)
2. What are my objectives? Specifically, what do I hope to accomplish?
3. How will I know when I have accomplished them? (evaluation)

When you have thoughtful answers to these questions, you have the nucleus for any funding request.

Let me first illustrate this thought process though an example taken from program planning done prior to seeking support for a re-entry women's internship program.

> **Problem Statement**
>
> The Volunteer Center is seeing increasing numbers of older women who are unable to successfully re-enter the job market due to their lack of recent job experience and low self-esteem.
>
> • **Program Idea:** Initiate a contracted internship program providing 3 month structured volunteer activity aimed at training and confidence building.
>
> • **Objectives:** To assist 100 women in reaching their employment goals through structured internships which provide confidence building and job experience and access.
>
> • **Evaluation:** A minimum of 100 women will complete their prescribed internship with 80% of them successful in reaching their employment goals by one month after the completion of their internship.

Your Plan to Solve the Problem

Let's look more carefully at each component:

- Through what means do you plan to solve the problem? (Program Idea)

Program Idea and Program Objectives

The informed funder will want to know why you have selected your particular method of addressing the problem This is your opportunity to show your awareness of other programs of a similar nature, their program methods and success, or any problems emanating from their models. Substantiating your reasons for selecting the model gives the potential funder a feeling that you are knowledgeable about your field. This, in turn, gives them a greater sense of security that you are a good risk for funding, thus increasing your chances of getting to **Yes!**

What You Hope to Accomplish

- **What are your objectives?**

If you have defined a problem, your objectives should offer some relief to that problem. If, for instance, your problem is a high incidence of drug use by teenagers in your school district, then the objective of your program should be the reduction of the incidence of drug abuse among children in that school district. If the problem is unemployment, then an objective would be the reduction of that unemployment.

One common problem pointed out to me by many funders is that often requests fail to distinguish between the means and the ends, between the program (methods) and the objectives.

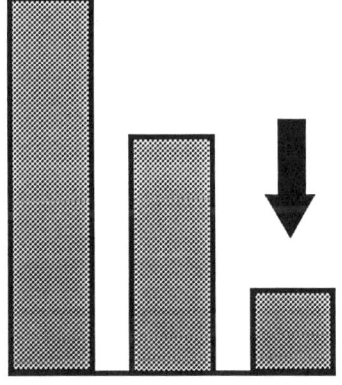

23

Thus many proposals read like these:

> "The purpose of this proposal is to establish a support group for potential high school drop-outs in the Dublin school district."

> "The objective of this program is to initiate a program to conduct early screening for Melanoma, a deadly form of skin cancer."

The problem with these objectives is that they do not speak of outcomes. How will a funder know if you made any difference with lowering the number of drop-outs or lowering the incidence of critical stages of melanoma? The fact that you have established a service or program does not tell a funder whether you have helped to solve the problem you have defined.

Simply working at a problem is not good enough. As a recent book title says, <u>Meaning Well Is Not Enough.</u>

Examples of **good objective statements** would be:

Simply working at a problem is not good enough

> "The objective of this program is to lower the incidence of high school drop-outs in our district from the current 35% to 20% of the entering freshman class by June, 1992."

> "The objective of this program is to have no reported deaths from melanoma during the three year screening program at the company."

Program Idea and Program Objectives

I am constantly amazed at the number of organizations that never define where they want to go and what they hope to accomplish. Some folks claim that the pressure is less when you are not holding yourself to any established goals and objectives. My view is quite different. It seems to me that the reason so many nonprofit leaders and organizations burn out is because they do not set clear, reasonable goals which can be celebrated and rewarded at their completion.

Organizations getting to **Yes** are adept at setting clear goals.

Program Evaluation

- **How will I know when I have accomplished my objectives?** (Evaluation)

   Sophisticated funders will ask the hard question, "How will you know if this program is successful?" We in the social sciences like to waffle on this question, mumbling such statements as, "How can we possibly know if our intervention was the determining factor in an individual's change?" or "We cannot afford (nor do we value the involvement of) sophisticated evaluation systems."

   What I have learned over the years is that if I am having difficulty in determining what criteria to use in evaluating a program, it is almost always due to the fact that my objectives are not specific enough.

25

I must therefore do further thinking in that area.

Another problem we often have in this area is that our evaluations tend to be mostly subjective in nature. Subjective evaluations usually tell you how people feel about a program, but seldom deal with concrete results. Subjective evaluations (e.g., how your clients liked the program and what they thought they learned or what key people in the community say about your service and its need) can be extremely effective with less sophisticated funders; in fact, they can have more impact than the academic approach.

The important point is to understand clearly what your funder needs in the way of an evaluation of the program. Nearly all funders, including individuals, want answers to the questions, "Were our money or our resources used wisely?" and "To what end?" Determine at the outset of your relationship with a potential funder what they will be needing in the way of an evaluation. If the funder sends out an independent evaluator, it is very important that you have clearly determined what the objectives are.

Program Idea and Program Objectives

Concluding Thoughts

Thinking through all of these issues surrounding the program idea, your objectives and evaluation are critical before making contact with a funder. But I learned through experience that you must remain flexible as you listen to the funder's hesitations or suggestions for modifications. I am convinced that often our requests were successful because we had not only carefully thought through our proposed service but also were open to funder suggestions, if we could maintain the integrity of our program while accommodating their interests.

Remember: It is the perfect match of the funder's needs and your needs that will eventually get you to **Yes!**

Planning and Preparation

It has been said (and I can heartily attest to it) that successful fund raising is 90% preparation and planning.

We are often so desperate for money that we like to compress this preparation period and get on to "the ask." Asking, however, when you have not thought through your proposal, when you do not have presentable materials to share and when you haven't screened for appropriate funders is often a frustrating experience, at best.

☐

Tips in Planning and Preparation Stages of the Proposal

Chapter 3 covered the essence of your proposal: the problem you are addressing and the solutions you bring to that need. There are many other areas of planning and preparation that you need to attend to before writing your proposal. These include the **budget, timing issues and future funding.**

Getting To Yes In Fund Raising

The Budget: After designing your program, you must ask: "How much will it cost our organization to carry out this new or enhanced program?" Funding sources will have a variety of requirements for budget reporting but generally you will want to realistically project program costs and present them in an acceptable accounting style. You will generally be safe if you prepare a budget with 2 components: Personnel and Non-personnel.

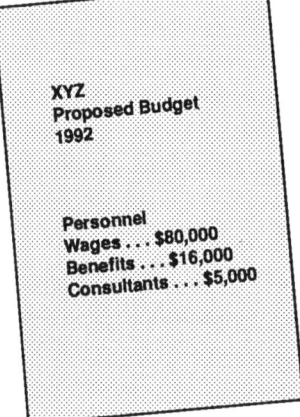

The **personnel** area of the budget will indicate:

- wages and salaries
- fringe benefits
- consultants and contract services
- volunteer/donated time

A word about volunteer time. I would highly recommend the inclusion of volunteer time and its projected value. (See appendix for the Karn method of calculating volunteer time.) By reporting this value, you will more clearly demonstrate the actual cost of providing this service. You will also lower the percentage cost of the full program that you are seeking from your donor. For example, if your program actual dollar cost is $10,000 and you can demonstrate that there is $5,000 of donated time, the total cost of running the program would be $15,000. If you ask the funder for $5,000, you will be asking for one-third, not one-half of the support. Also, showing donated support is very impressive to a funder who is attempting

Planning and Preparation

to assess their risk in supporting your request.

It is important to know that nonprofit budgets, on average, will have 80% of their budget in personnel costs. (Some funders do not know this and may comment on your high personnel costs. Time to educate!)

Non-personnel items in the budget generally consist of:

space costs (or donated value)

equipment (leased or purchased)

consumable supplies

travel

phone

training

insurance

printing

misc.

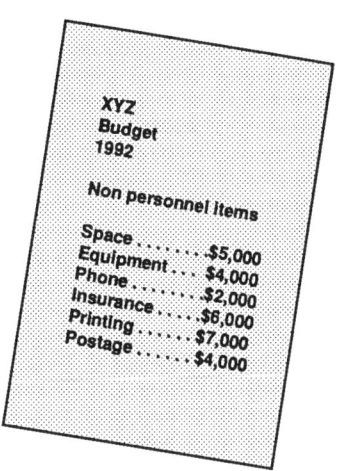

XYZ
Budget
1992

Non personnel items

Space $5,000
Equipment ... $4,000
Phone $2,000
Insurance $6,000
Printing $7,000
Postage $4,000

A good part of our success at getting to **Yes** in fund raising could be attributed to the significant amount of in-kind donations we had (space, equipment and furniture, printing, etc.). Reporting all of these services or items is very impressive to funders. It truly amazes me that very few organizations take the time to calculate and reflect this on their budget proposal. If they do, it is frequently a figure lost in the narrative.

Timing Issues: Most foundations or large corporations need a 6 month turn around time to determine if they can

31

Getting To Yes In Fund Raising

support you. Many also have cut off times for consideration within a year. You need to be cognizant of these times in your planning.

It is frequently helpful to apply during the first quarter or first half of their fiscal year as often they have fewer dollars to distribute at the end of their year.

Remember: Always research the funder's fiscal year and act accordingly.

Future Funding: Another part of planning will involve determining an answer to the inevitable question, "How will you fund this after we no longer support this effort?"

In my experience the answers usually revolves around one of these responses:

1. "We won't need any additional support (capital item) except for maintenance which will be obtained through user fees, etc."

2. "If this program is successful, we will provide it on a contracted basis to another organization or we will establish a reasonable sliding scale fee for users of the service." (Along with this plan, you may want to propose a scholarship fund for those unable to pay for the service.)

3. "If this service is successful, we will develop a plan to generate annual gifts from members of service clubs, churches and individuals."

You know your potential re-

Planning and Preparation

sources. **Do some creative thinking!** I must confess that often I said the above with my fingers crossed. But more often than not, these sketchy future funding plans did materialize, making me a firm believer in this philosophy:

If you truly develop an excellent, needed service or program, there *are* sources to support it as long as the need continues to exist. Keeping this mind-set opens your creative juices for funding solutions that will enable you to get to **Yes**!

☐

Tips for Putting Together an Agency Prospectus

In your planning and preparation, one of the most helpful tools to develop is an agency prospectus, an attractive folder of key information on your organization. (Tip: I recommend that organizations use the type of folder which becomes its own file — for obvious reasons.)

A prospectus may contain:

- 1 page history of the organization
- awards you have received
- unsolicited letters of praise
- summary of goals/long range plans
- brochures and any attractive information on the organization
- charts and graphs showing growth, number of clients, etc.
- agency's current year budget
- list of board and staff members

Getting To Yes In Fund Raising

- other "show and tell" items

This great tool can be readily adapted to meet the interests and needs of any potential funder you will be seeing. Having attractive visuals to share can calm the nerves of many individuals attempting to sell their organization. Funders generally love this professional, quick, visual way to get in touch with your program.

I have recommended to organizations that they seek a volunteer with an artistic flair to design the prospectus folder and to pull together and/or develop attractive materials and arrange them for presentation.

There is no question in my mind that an attractive, informative prospectus can have significant influence in getting the funder to **Yes**!

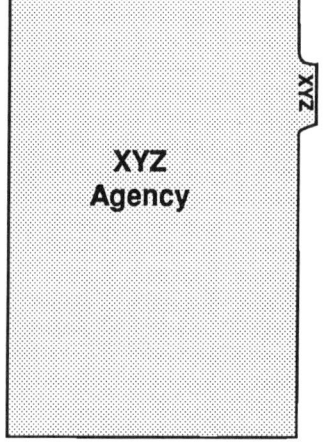

The valuable agency prospectus

Tips in Researching Appropriate Funders

A major factor in getting to **Yes** is to be knocking on the right door. Therefore, much of your planning and preparation time will be spent researching funding sources or individuals who are most likely to give you support.

Living in cities such as San Francisco, New York, Washington D.C. or Cleveland will give you a great advantage as these areas have excellent Foundation Center Libraries for researching all types of foundation and corporation giving in relationship to your interests and needs. Many

Planning and Preparation

large metropolitan or university libraries also have collections of resource directories which will give you guidance in answer to your questions:

- What corporations or foundations have an interest in our type of organization or program?
- What is the average size of their grant?
- When do I apply and what is their application procedure?
- Are they conservative or progressive in their approach to funding?
- What percentage of grant seekers receive funding?
- What is their granting cycle?
- Etc.

Once you are set on your programs and budget needs, you will need some dedicated research time to locate possible funding sources.

Often anxious seekers of funds blitz the funding world with their request rather than personalizing their approach. What they need to do is to indicate that through research, they have become aware that the funder has an interest in their proposed area of work. Non-targeted letters most often get the "Sorry, but good luck" response, with no opportunity for further discussions.

Tip: I discovered that many funders in a specified geographic area meet on a regular basis to discuss, among other things, the requests coming to them. So, a word to the wise, "Don't blitz funders and expect them to think you have done your homework - even if the word processor makes it appear so."

Types of Foundation and Corporate Giving Structures

Understanding the types of foundation and corporate giving is important knowledge in assisting you in your search for just the right donor. The following descriptions may be useful to distinguish the features of private and community foundations and corporate giving programs.

The term "private foundation" is a legal classification defined by the Internal Revenue Code. These foundations typically receive their funds from a single donor, corporation, or family. They are governed by a self-perpetuating board of directors who make grant decisions and set policy.

Private foundations whose boards are composed primarily of the family members or business associates of the original donor are called **"family foundations."** In my experience, I found it initially difficult to get to **Yes** with family foundations as many of them have a long personal history of working with organizations or schools with which family members are involved. Also their interests can change at the whim of a family member; as an outsider, it is very difficult to keep abreast of them. After we had some

Planning and Preparation

success and developed a good reputation with other foundations and corporations, it seemed easier to break through to these family foundations. In fact, once into their funding circle, we found them an excellent source of project support.

Some profit-making corporations establish private foundations to manage their charitable giving programs. These **"corporate foundations"** generally take on the name of the donor corporation (e.g., Clorox Foundation), and have boards composed of senior executives of the corporation. Corporate foundations often restrict their granting to the geographic areas in which the corporation has plants or other facilities, or in which corporate employees reside. My experience has been that getting to **Yes** was somewhat enhanced by getting to personally know the director of the foundation.

All private foundations, be they family, independent, or corporate, are governed by a payout requirement set by law. They must distribute 5% of their assets for charitable purposes each year. They must also file an annual information return (Form 990 PF) with the IRS. Among the information required on the 990 PF is a complete list of all grants awarded, application deadlines and procedures, and a list of board members of the foundation. These returns, by law, are public information and are available for free public use.

Community foundations are established under a separate classification of

Form 990

Grants Awarded
Application deadlines
Board Members

Getting To Yes In Fund Raising

the tax code and typically focus their granting on a specific city, county or other geographic region. Their endowments are made up of contributions, bequests or trusts from a number of individuals or corporations. Boards of community foundations are generally not self-perpetuating; appointments to the boards are made by outside agencies or institutions.

Because they are independent of donor control, community foundations enjoy some special privileges under the tax laws. They are exempt from the payout requirement and are not required to file the form 990 PF.

My personal experience with several community foundations was that it was initially difficult to get their attention, but persistence paid off and getting personally acquainted with the foundation staff was extremely useful.

☐

Corporate Giving Programs

For-profit corporations, by law, may take a tax deduction for charitable contributions up to a ceiling of 10% of their pre-tax profits. Some corporations use a private foundation to manage their charitable grants or they may give directly through their public affairs, public relations, community affairs or other department. Those corporations which do their giving directly are not required to file public information returns on their giving programs and therefore may or may not be listed in funding directories.

Planning and Preparation

The best way to get a relationship with corporate donors, if you do not have a personal contact, is to work through any of their employees who are familiar with and supportive of your program. They can have access to very useful information and can serve as an important internal advocate for you.

Nationally, the trend is to increasingly tie employees' interests and volunteer activities with the corporations' donated dollars. Therefore, I would reiterate my recommendation of involving corporate and business people as volunteers or board members in your organization so that they can make these valuable contacts on your behalf.

Concluding Thoughts

Planning and preparation is often tedious and time consuming work, so perhaps you may want to keep this quote handy to keep you motivated:

"Spectacular Achievement is always preceded by — Unspectacular preparation!"[1]

Footnotes

1. This quote was taken from Zig Ziglar's <u>Secrets of Closing The Sale</u>, p. 168. The quote is by Dr. Robert Schuller, author of <u>Move Ahead with Possibility Thinking.</u>

Preliminary Interest of Funder

Means of Determining a Funder's Interest

Once your research has ascertained that a person, foundation, or corporation may be a potential source of funding, you now become a detective. The more you know about your potential funder, organizationally and individually, the better your approach will be.

How does one go about further determining a funder's interest without putting her/himself in jeopardy of hearing an early "No"?

At this stage, you cannot be certain that there will be a mutual interest until you can communicate with them via phone, letter or in person. Let's take a brief look at each method to determine its potential strengths and liabilities.

☐

Phone Contact

I would be remiss if I did not first alert you to the fact that sometimes a foundation or corporation will request that your first communication be in writing. This is done so that they can save staff time by screening many inappropriate requests at this stage. Honor that.

If at all possible, however, I would suggest that you have some verbal communication with a staff person at the foundation or corporation office. It may only be to ask that they send you the latest information on their interests and suggested format for submitting material. If appropriate, I also like to succinctly ask these questions:

- **Will the upcoming funding period be a good time to submit our request?**

  I ask this because often a foundation or corporation will simply be holding over requests that they liked from the former funding period. They may not be planning to select any new ones that session and may not tell you this, unless you ask.

- **Does the written material you will be sending us (or that I have received) reflect your current funding interests?**

Preliminary Interest of Funder

Many small foundations send dated material (e.g., an annual statement that is 2-4 years old). We once went through the process of a lengthy written proposal to a foundation, only to find out that they had changed their focus. We were basing our match on outdated information.

- **Does your foundation/corporation allow an in-person pre-proposal interview?**

Surprisingly, a number of funders indicate that they will either speak briefly with you on the phone or see you in their office for a maximum of 30 minutes. I found the latter to be the case only if you were known by the funding source through previous work with them.

I would caution you that after you have asked this question, you should be prepared to share the essence of your proposed program, its cost and how you want them to contribute to it. You do not want to "tell all" because too much information may lead them to respond with an immediate "no interest" on the phone.

What seasoned fund raisers become adept at doing during this stage is finding out as much as possible about the funder's interests so that they can modify or assess their program's potential to fit with the funder's interest.

Generally the folks you speak with during this initial contact are office managers or receptionists or, in the case of corporations, community relations staff. As with any office, some seem very well trained to give no specific information and to be rather discouraging. Others are very informative, pleasant and helpful. My suggestion would be to sense how much information they are at liberty to give you and to get it. Naturally, you should also be friendly and professional. (Their comments on how you handled yourself on the phone may come back to haunt you!)

Occasionally, in a small office, the foundation director or corporate giving officer answers your call. I'll never forget how dumbfounded I was the first time that happened to me. I remember hanging up I was so stunned. Now I see this as a great opportunity to get acquainted and to find out as much as I can as to whether we might have a match.

One last thought. Sometimes it is best to hear "No" at this stage as it may well save you hours of time developing a proposal to an unlikely source. If you are doing adequate research on sources of funds, you will be hearing or sensing "No" quite frequently.

Preliminary Interest of Funder

But, as some wise person once said:

> "Don't get discouraged; it is often the last key in the bunch that opens the lock."[1]

- **How long does it generally take your foundation (corporation) to come to a decision once a full proposal is submitted?**

Getting a sense of the timing will enable you to plan more accurately a potential start date for your new service. If they indicate that the time is four months, you should mark the date on a tickler file. If you have not heard from them by shortly after that time, you can communicate with them by saying, "I understood that you would be making a decision by this time and I am calling to determine the **current status of my proposal.**" I found that this phrase came in handy when I needed information on my proposal and did not want to appear too pushy.

- **Who makes funding decisions in your organization?**

It is useful to discover whether the staff members make decisions up to certain dollar amounts and if and when the Board has the final say. This was very useful in one particular instance when we wanted to get a grant within a 3 month time period and we knew that grants over $25,000 went

45

Approval Amount

through a lengthy approval process at the Board level of the institution. We requested $24,500 and had the money 2 months earlier than if we had requested $25,250. There was also the chance that the board might not approve the staff recommendation.

There may be many other questions that are important for you to ask at this time. The important thing is to ask them now. You do not want to be surprised later with any information that was essential to know to enhance your chances for funding.

☐

Letter of Intent

It was Pascal in 1665 who wrote to a friend, **"I have only made this letter rather long because I have not had the time to make it short."**[2]

My first suggestion in the letter of intent is to make it as short as possible. It should showcase the credibility of your organization, share the broad concept of your proposed program, show evidence of your awareness of the funder's interests and indicate your desire to further discuss the possibility of working together. If you have not had a chance to personally discuss your proposed work with the funder, you do not want to tell them too much before picking up clues as to their focus.

If your organization is not known by the funder, it is extremely important that

Preliminary Interest of Funder

this letter be written in such a way that the funder is intrigued with who you are and what you are doing. Many funders have shared with me how often these first impression letters are poorly written, thus lowering their chances of getting noticed in any way but negatively. I would surmise that many excellent programs are screened out at this stage because they don't understand the importance of this beginning step.

My goal with a letter of intent is to get the "green light" to continue or to commence our discussions determining if we have a match. The foundation uses the letter of intent to screen many requests from the hundreds they receive.

□

Pre-Proposal Interview

The ideal manner to first connect with a funder is in a brief face to face meeting. When trying to arrange a meeting, I generally say something like, "I will be in the vicinity of your corporation on_____. I would love an opportunity to come by to briefly get acquainted and share with you an innovative program idea I have in _____" (obviously something in which the funder has a major interest).

If the visit is denied, what generally happens is that they give you an opportunity to discuss it with them on the phone. So again, be prepared to succinctly share your idea, your needs and then LISTEN. They will be giving you valuable clues as to your possibility of establishing a match with them.

47

Getting To Yes In Fund Raising

I remember one experience when I went to a pre-proposal session for an arts group. We wanted money to hire a staff person to raise funds for us. (Wouldn't we all!) What we heard when we listened was that they would not be interested in hiring a fund raiser. Rather, they were interested in proposals that would increase audience development so that the organizations would be increasing their earned income. In many ways we were trying to accomplish the same thing.

We learned that to be successful in receiving funds from this foundation, we would need to have our focus be audience development. (This, by the way, was never stated in their literature.) We returned to our organization and developed a proposal to hire a person for two years to assist the organization in increasing its earned income through audience development. The grant was successful and the organization solved its funding crisis. Had we not had this pre-proposal visit, I am quite certain that we would not have received the grant.

☐

> XYZ Theater Proposal
>
> Increased Earned Income through Audience Development

Concluding Remarks

One of the keys in getting to **Yes** is the research and detective work we do to see if the funder may have an interest in us and how we might position ourselves, or word our request, to further our chances of a positive response.

☐

Preliminary Interest of Funder

Footnotes:

1. Great Quotations, Inc. Ziz Ziglar's Favorite Quotations, 1989.
2. Lord, James Gregory. The Raising of Money, p. ix.

6

Proposal Preparation

If you have not taken a course or read books on proposal writing, I would strongly advise that you do so. The intent of this chapter is to share proposal preparation hints which may be the factors that tip the scale to **Yes** for your organization.

Making Your Proposal Stand Out

Remember: funders have numerous requests daily from worthy organizations with creative, effective new programs. What can you do to make yours stand out among the rest?

My first simple suggestion is to have it neatly prepared on a laser or other high quality printer. Hopefully your computer or word processor has a spell check. Use it!

Many funders have shared their concern regarding the appearance of proposals coming across their desk. It need not take excess funds to have your proposal attractive. If you do not have the latest equipment, find a business willing to run your proposal on their equipment. (Easy for them, marvelous for you!) And while you are there, you might ask them to keep you in mind when they discard this equipment for updated, upscaled models.

A word of caution for proposals that may look overdone (e.g., fancy covers, multicolored graphs and charts, etc.). Some funders are concerned over the expense involved in very slick presentations. Many funders have also shared their less than enthusiastic response when it is obvious that an organization hired a consultant to do the proposal.

Because I am aware of many funders' response to this type of consultant, I always tell my clients that my purpose in working with them is to teach and guide them through the process so that the skill will remain within the organization and there is no further need for a consultant.

Another possible problem with the entrance of a professional fund developer into an organization is that it is almost always followed by board member sighs, "Phew! Now we don't have to worry about

Proposal Preparation

money any more."

Another tip for having your proposal or solicitation letter stand out is to put a personal note (yellow sticky is great) on the proposal to anyone you know or even have casually met.

Once I submitted a proposal to a major corporate foundation in San Francisco. I must admit I felt less than optimistic about our chances since most of their grants went to places such as Stanford University. Just before sending out the proposal, I put a small yellow sticky note on the cover letter - a friendly hello to one of their program officers I had causally met at a meeting several months earlier. After I got a call from this man, I thought to myself, "Maybe the secretary saw this note and automatically sent him the proposal sensing we were friendly acquaintances." One doesn't always know, but I tried it a number of times later and it always worked.

So I offer the yellow sticky tip for enhancing your chances of being noticed and getting to **Yes**.

☐

Writing a Good Introduction/ Proposal Summary

Here again, brevity, clarity and energy are the keys. For many who screen proposals, this one page summary will be the key factor in whether this organization is seriously considered for funding. Many funders have indicated that if they are hesitant after reading the summary, they most often do not continue reading.

53

Getting To Yes In Fund Raising

It is suggested that you write the summary page after the entire proposal has been completed. To test its effectiveness you should ask these three questions:

- When reading it, can you *feel* the energy of the organization?
- Can you ascertain a clear idea of the problem, the proposed solution and what is needed to achieve the goal(s)?
- Do you sense that this is a credible agency, well suited to carry out the work?

Clear, Concise and Alive Writing

Just as with the summary statement, the full proposal should meet the test for clarity, brevity and energy. On occasion when the executive or program director has a writing style that causes people to nod off, they should consider collecting all the material for the proposal and handing it to an excellent writer to prepare the draft.

Innovators of ideas may not be the best writers. You won't often get to **Yes** with a great idea and poor communication skills.

Be Aware of Jargon

Most often funders will not be experts in your field. Thus, heavy use of your field's jargon (writing about your PRN's and your STZ's) will only frustrate and discourage a potential funder.

54

Proposal Preparation

Have an Outsider Critique your Proposal

Since your potential funders may not be knowledgeable about your organization or your field, I find it particularly helpful to have someone outside of the agency read and critique the request letter or proposal.

Select an honest critique. Praise is nice, but that's not what is helpful at this juncture.

☐

Include Credibility Information in the Appendix

Many funders will give guidelines regarding their interest in seeing any letters of recommendation, newspaper articles about your organization, brochures, etc. My suggestion is to follow their advice. But if they simply say they don't want information in the proposal, I always suggest putting together an attractive appendix which includes selected pieces to enhance your organization's image.

If you include marvelous *unsolicited* letters from clients or key community people, or newspaper articles, use a highlighter to surface the important phrases or sentences you want them to read.

My theory has always been that even if they toss this section into the circular file, they may see and remember how supported, endorsed and wonderful you appear to be.

For some organizations, I have suggested that they deliver or send their attractive agency prospectus in a self-file folder. It may become the basis of information the funder collects on an organization. If the funder has explicitly stated "No additional information should be attached to the proposal", I suggest that you send it or present it to them at a different time.

Connect your Program to their Area of Interest and their Ability to Support

Make certain that you have accurate information on the funders' interests and then continually tie their interests to yours. Also be certain that you are in their ball park on the amount of money requested. The foundation or corporation staff may be very helpful to you as you put your proposal together, but you need to ask.

It is advisable to have a specific amount to ask for and a plan for how the remainder will be obtained. If you are a new organization to them, they will be less likely to give the lead gift or one reflecting the top end of their giving scale.

I encourage your continued conversation with potential funders.

Most beginning fund raisers tend to privately speculate on most of these issues. Perhaps this is why we hear "No" so often in our initial attempts to seek funding.

Remember - The funder may like your proposed program, but if the amount requested is out of line with their ability

Proposal Preparation

and history of giving, you may not receive the **Yes** you were desiring.

☐

Write A Cover Letter

A brief, non-attached cover letter is, I believe, the final touch to an attractive, professional proposal. It is the time to say thank you for their consideration and to encourage their continued contact with you during their review process.

☐

Concluding Comments

As you may have noted, all of the above tips are primarily based on your presentation, not the content of your program. This is not to discount the program's extreme importance. I have made the assumption that you do have an excellent solution to a problem you have cited.

I contend that, all things being equal (i.e., all agency programs being well run and dealing effectively with real needs), it is often the presentation of these ideas that influences what requests will get to **Yes.**

☐

7

Patience and Persistence

Assuming that your written request is in the mail (usually postmarked at 4:59 P.M.), your next step in the process is the waiting game. There are 5 tips I would share for this anxious time.

☐

1. Did the Proposal Arrive?

Unless you hand carried and delivered it to the funder personally, I would always recommend doing a return guarantee notice from the post office or allowing several days to go by and making a call to determine that it has arrived.

If you are anxious to stay in touch, you may want to use this excuse to make a call to them. Remember, there is a fine line between a pest and someone who strategically gets the information they need to enhance their chance of success.

☐

2. Send Updates and Keep Your Organization in Front of Funder

I do a great deal of co-training with funders. Often in our sessions they indicate how much they appreciate receiving any new and updated information that may reflect on the proposal or any specific information or news articles about your organization.

As Carmella Johnson, Contributions Manager, Clorox Corporation, says in our trainings, "Your agency continually comes to our mind if we see or hear new things about you."

We as fund seekers must keep the funders apprised of our activities. They cannot be proactive in this area since they are dealing with so many organizations.

☐

3. Ask For "the Status of My Proposal"

This useful phrase can help you track what is happening to your request if you have not heard anything for a long period.

I have always operated on the philosophy that "no news is generally good news" (i.e., your proposal has not been rejected, yet!). Often, however, in businesses or corporations where there are no deadlines or any specific process for review, you may need to bring your organization's request to their attention.

A most frustrating experience in fund raising is when you are strung along be-

Patience and Persistence

cause of the funder's discomfort in telling you "No". If I sense that this may be the case, I try to educate them (gently!) as to the frustration in this. I would much prefer to hear "No" in a timely fashion, than wait endless days hoping for a **Yes** that never comes.

☐

4. Handling a Rejection Letter at This Stage

If you receive a rejection notice after your initial inquiry, this primarily is due to the funder's sense that your interests and theirs do not match.

If you receive a rejection after the written proposal phase, it may indicate one of several things:

- There was important information about the funders interests, etc. of which you were unaware. (You really are not a good match with this foundation's interests and stipulations.)

- There were other organizations or proposals in the same field which appeared stronger to the funder.

- You are new to the funder and they are not convinced to take a risk with you.

- Your organization is unstable or undergoing major staff changes.

- They have already distributed all of their money for this year.

What you will generally receive is a polite form letter which in essence says,

61

"Sorry, but our best wishes to you in the future."

My advice, if you are miffed by this rejection, is to call the funder and ask if you can speak briefly to an appropriate person who can share honestly with you why your proposal was turned down. Funders say that surprisingly very few people ever do this. In your early stages of fund development, this can be your best learning experience.

If you call the funder, you may wish to inquire about the following:

- Will there be future opportunities for funding with them and how they may suggest changing your proposal to more fully coincide with their interests, etc.?

- Was there anything in your program or your presentation about which they could give you constructive feedback?

- Could there be an opportunity to briefly meet in person to get acquainted and mutually share your interests and needs? (This should only be done if you sense a potential future relationship with this funder.)

FUTURE OPPORTUNITIES

FEEDBACK

BRIEF MEETING

This above activity is really the beginning of the exercise of persistence. You must cultivate the quality of persistence if you wish to experience success in getting to **Yes** in fund raising.

Patience and Persistence

Remember: Failure has been correctly identified as the path of least "persistence."[1]

5. Thanking Funder for Their Consideration

The last thing you want to do after receiving a rejection on your proposal is to write them a thank you letter. And, according to funders I know, it's not done often. In fact, one funder said, "I can count on one hand the number of thank you letters I have received after we turned down a grant request and ...I can name exactly which agencies they are!" It is apparently such a rare phenomenon that they don't forget you when you take the time to thank them for their efforts in reviewing your proposal.

I am a great believer in recognition and appreciation (see chapter 11) and it would appear that most folks are missing a golden opportunity to become an organization that is remembered. It may very well enhance your future efforts at getting to **Yes**.

Footnotes:

1. Great Quotations, Inc. <u>Zig Ziglar's Favorite Quotations</u>, 1989, p.57.

Persuasive Presentations to Funding Sources

"You won't have a second chance to make a first impression"

If you have the good fortune of having a funding source call you to set up a personal visit, you should take time for a little celebration before planning this presentation. In my experience, you are well on your way to a **Yes**. The funder has reviewed your written proposal and has obviously found merit in it. Now they want to check out you!

You have no doubt heard that people fund people, not causes (i.e., people give to people they know or to people with whom they can easily relate or connect). Therefore, if you are an unknown to the funder at this point, you need to think through this meeting with great care. As the old saying goes, "You won't have a second chance to make a first impression."

Tips

Establishing a Personal Link with the Funder

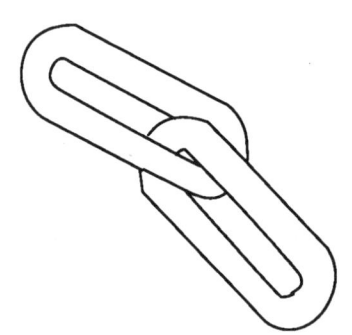

The following are some tips to help you make that all important connection with the funder.

□

In the first few minutes of "chit chat," aim to uncover something you and the funder share in common (e.g., a person you both know, an activity or sport in which you are both involved, personal experiences that connect you, etc.). It has always been amazing to me how much more relaxed and positive the ensuing discussion is after this connection is made.

I could share numerous examples but several outstanding ones come to mind. On one occasion we were visiting a funder about our women's re-entry internship program. A connection was made quickly when the funder shared the dilemma and stress his wife had undergone when she tried to return to the job market after a long absence. There was an instant bonding of understanding between us and I knew we would get to yes. When we did, it was a jubilant celebration, expecially since we had been turned down previously by 18 potential funders.

Remember: It was the same program, but we had finally connected with the appropriate funder who also shared a *personal* interest in program.

Another example that stands out in my mind was when the foundation director came to see us. Believe me, we were petrified! During our get acquainted time,

Persuasive Presentations to Funding Sources

he indicated that he was still very active as a volunteer with the Boy Scouts of America. When he asked us what a volunteer center did, I fortunately had enough wit about me to recall an example. I used the match we had recently made between a young man working to become an Eagle Scout and some service needs in our community.

Looking back on that moment, I knew we would get to **Yes**. His demeanor and interest perked up immediately and we went on to have a wonderful sharing. As it turned out, it was the first grant we ever received. Nothing has ever been as hard since then!

They must buy you before they buy your ideas!

So...aim to establish a connection early in your session. As all sales training will tell you:

They must buy you before they buy your ideas!

☐

Dress Like the People You are Going to See

Regardless of what attire is appropriate for you organizational setting, determine the dress code of your funder and follow it. I have read that it is always important to **dress to blend, not offend.** After all, how can you influence someone if you have already offended them?

Even if the funders are coming to your setting, you will want to look as much like them as possible or they will feel very uncomfortable in your environment. Think about yourself - What kind of people do you bond with most easily?...That's right, the ones that look and think like you!

Remember: You are trying to create an environment that is most conducive to getting to **Yes**.

☐

Try to Have the Meeting in Your Setting

Your "dog and pony show" will obviously be much easier to stage at your own facility, so encourage them to come to you. Arrange a time when your agency is most active and interesting. Seeing the actual work you do with clients is the most powerful way to share your story.

If you are just a business office (e.g., as in the case of a theater group), you will want to invite them to see your product. If they cannot come, it may be helpful for you to have a short video to show them. While at the volunteer center, we had our local cable TV station produce a 10 minute video for us. One of its best uses turned out, unexpectedly, to be with funders.

☐

Be Prepared, Organized, Flexible, Brief and Professional

This may sound a bit like the Boy Scout oath, but I can't emphasize enough how important each of these characteristics is towards making an excellent impression.

I can look back on my first years of fund raising and see how often we were lacking in one of these characteristics. It nearly always had a negative effect on our presentation.

Persuasive Presentations to Funding Sources

Several rules of thumb for beginning fund raisers:

- Overprepare, but listen for clues as to what will be appropriate to share at your session.

- Practice your presentation out loud and let someone critique it for you. It should be articulate and succinct without losing enthusiasm. (Easy to say, difficult to do.) Practice, practice, practice!

- Always ask ahead how much time you will have in your session and plan your presentation accordingly. People are very time conscious. Use it wisely. (When you notice them yawning as they peer down at their watches, you will know you have blown it!)

Find out in Advance What Questions will be Asked, and Who will be Present

When the funder calls to invite you for a visit, use this opportunity to ask them:

- how long the meeting will be,
- if they want you to make a formal presentation,
- who will be there from their organization (and anything you can find out about them),
- what questions they will be asking you,

69

- any written information they want you to bring,
- if you can bring additional people to the session (assuming it is at their office)

The bottom line: The more you know what to expect at the meeting, the more you will be on target with them. Foundation and corporate funders have shared with me that rarely do fund seekers ask these very appropriate questions.

If you are going to a business or corporation, it is advisable to find out as much as possible about the key person you need to influence. This is where board members "in the know" can help. You can make that all important personal connection considerably faster when you have done your homework in this area.

☐

Use Volunteers/ Clients to Present and Support Your Funding Request

As an Executive Director, I began to increasingly see my role as the orchestrator of these sessions, as opposed to the main speaker. Bringing along *enthusiastic, articulate* volunteers, including board members, can make an impact that no paid personnel can do no matter how charismatic they are. This is a perfect role for that incredible, fantastic volunteer who says "I'll do anything but ask for money". In most cases, they are very comfortable making presentations to funding sources where they are an applicant. I discovered that once they saw how fulfilling it was to influence funders to

Persuasive Presentations to Funding Sources

support their cause, asking from individuals became easier.

There is no question in my mind that one of our secrets to success in fundraising was the selective use of volunteers to tell our story.

Another highly effective way to sell your program is to have testimonials given by clients who have been impacted by the programs you offer. Again, hearing an unwed pregnant teen tell the story of how her life was turned around by an internship is very compelling, much more so than if that same story was told by a paid employee.

Studies on influence and sales have determined that people buy ideas, products, etc., 90% based on emotions, 10% based on logic.

Knowing this, we need to frame our questions, "How do you feel about it?" not, "What do you think about it?"

One caution. If you use volunteers and/or clients, make sure that you are very clear in your instructions. Also have at least one rehearsal. (I could tell a few horror stories here.)

☐

Utilize Various Types of Presentations

Even if we do our homework well and find out a good deal about the person(s) with whom we are meeting, we will most likely be unaware of how this person takes in information.

We know from learning theory that people are generally either auditory, visual or kinesthetic learners. (A quick way to determine which they are is to listen to their language. Do they say "I hear", "I see" or "I feel" most often?)

I generally recommend that you develop your presentation with all three learning methods in mind. For instance, don't just talk about your program, also show pictures, a video or something visual along with your presentation. For the kinesthetic learners, getting them on your site may be very important for them to really feel the organization.

With practice, you will soon be very adept at this as it will just come naturally to you. Initially, however, you may need to think through your style of presentation to be certain that someone with any learning style will be able to understand what you are attempting to impart.

Influence of Voice Inflection/ Body Language

Most people spend their preparation time in selecting the words to be used in a presentation. Perhaps we all need an occasional reminder of this well known study:

> The Impact of Our Presentations
>
> 7% - The words we use
>
> 38% - The way we say them
>
> 55% - Our body language

Persuasive Presentations to Funding Sources

Know How You Stand After Your Meeting

It is very important to understand where you stand at the end of this meeting. If the funder doesn't offer you this information, it is imperative for you to ask:

- "How do we stand with you (the funder) at this time?" (i.e., what chance do we have for funding and how much can we anticipate receiving?)
- "When will you have an answer for us?"
- "Is there anything we need to send you or do at this time?"

Concluding Comments

In my experience, they will often give you an answer which is prefaced by, "We can't say anything for certain until the board meets, however, ..."

☐

During this personal contact and presentation phase of fund raising, you will begin to understand why many refer to fund raising as an art.

Fund raising is:

- the **art** of targeting donors who have the perfect match with your needs and interest
- the **art** of cultivating these potential funders

73

- the **art** of making such a compeling presentation of *your clients' needs* that you are certain to be on you way to

Getting to Yes in Fund Raising.

☐

Patience and Persistence (Again!)

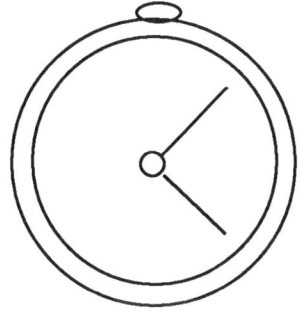

After making your presentation to the funder, you will enter another round of patience. Generally this time period is shorter since many proposals have been screened out by now. You are often waiting for the meeting of the funder's board or council to make their final decisions.

As indicated in chapter 8, you will frequently have a fairly good idea of the recommendation that the funder will be making. I generally ask the funder when the board meeting will be held and how long after it meets will we be notified of the decision. Some foundations and corporations will encourage you to call the following day to get the final decision since it often takes them upwards to two weeks to officially notify you.

☐

If You Are Turned Down

If you are told "no go" at this time, major depression (and an occasional bit of anger) is apt to set in. You have put in an enormous number of hours in your written and oral presentations and at this moment, all seems for naught. What are your options at this time?

- Go home and cry a lot!
- Call the funder and tell them there must have been a mistake!
- Decide you will never fund raise again

or

- Call the program officer with whom you worked, express your disappointment and ask at least these 2 questions:

> 1. **Can you give us some honest feedback on why our proposal was not funded?**
> 2. **What if anything can we do to get to Yes?**

Question 2 is probably the most important question I ever ask funders who have turned down our request. One example sticks out in my mind.

In the late 1980's I was anxious for our organization to hire someone to do research on the impact that increasing

Patience and Persistence (Again!)

numbers of working people were having on volunteering. Our first proposal was for $25,000 to do research in nonprofit organizations and corporations. When we were not funded, I was tremendously disappointed as I had thought we were getting to **Yes.**

Magic Question To Ask

I asked the magic question, "Is there anyway we could revise this proposal to get to **Yes** in your foundation?" They responded that their board had not been interested in funding the corporate research side of the proposal, but they had been very interested in looking at how nonprofit organizations were having to adjust their volunteer program to accommodate to the new working volunteers.

With this very helpful piece of information, I proceeded to re-think the proposal and during the next cycle, requested a $45,000 grant to study the nonprofit side. We not only received the full amount but later received a second grant to enable our researcher, Nora Silver, to write a book, <u>At The Heart, The New Volunteer Challenge to Community Organizations</u>.

That very important question - "Is there any way we can get to **Yes**?" - has not only opened up a funding opportunity in this situation but in many other areas during the last 16 years.

Remember: Others can stop you temporarily - you are the only one who can do it permanently[1]

☐

Getting To Yes In Fund Raising

Footnotes:

1. Great Quotations, Inc. <u>Zig Ziglar's Favorite Quotations,</u> p. 13.

10

Presentation of the Check (Pleased and Proud)

This is a very short - but sweet chapter. There is no feeling quite so wonderful as when you receive your nice check in a letter which says, "Congratulations, we have decided to fund your program in the amount of $_____."

All of the blood, sweat and tears seem worth while at this moment. The dream or vision of the program you wanted to start, the equipment that was desperately needed can now come to fruition. No feeling can quite match it. If you haven't felt it yet, hang in there. It is worth waiting for. And believe me, once you have experienced success, more will follow.

☐

Celebrate the News!

Early in my fund raising days, I remember having a grand celebration after learning of a grant of a mere $2,000. After all, many staff and volunteers had worked very hard and had no doubt heard many "Nos" before this.

After a few years we became very successful in receiving many large grants and I realized that we were no longer pausing to celebrate the moment. In fact, we had become rather blasé about the grants. **Yes** was something we had come to expect.

But we didn't always get to **Yes** and I began to sense some burnout and fatigue over our fund raising efforts. Remembering the great energy booster our little celebrations had been, I consciously reinstated them. They seemed to be the key to keeping paid and volunteer staff energized to continue to go through the sometimes tedious and tough job of seeking resources for the visions we held.

Remember: Pause to celebrate **Yes!**

□

Proliferation of Thank Yous and Perpetuation of the Contact

When I train in recognition, I title my workshop, <u>Creative Recognition - The Art of Letting Someone Know You Noticed.</u> Too often, however, recognition seems to be anything but creative. Often it is seen as a necessary obligation which must be performed to formally thank a funder or donor for their contribution. There is limited understanding of the phenomenal value and power that recognition gives both to its receiver and to the giver.

During my workshop I ask participants to recall their own experiences with recognition and then, as a group, to share what they learned about recognition from

Getting To Yes In Fund Raising

listening to these experiences. They invariably say:

Key Characteristics of Recognition

- There are many formal and informal ways to thank people.
- Recognition can be motivating, powerful, and energizing.
- Recognition can be very creative or very routine.
- Recognition is not done often.
- We frequently fall into the trap of wanting to give the kind of recognition we would like to receive, rather than considering what would be meaningful to the person.
- Sometimes recognition can really "miss the boat."
- Everyone likes and needs recognition.

We need to keep these simple truths in mind as we look at appropriate ways to thank our donors.

☐

Three Key Rules of Recognition for Donors

1. Find out what kind of recognition the funder expects, needs, likes—and do it!
2. Give recognition soon after the receipt of the gift.
3. Recognize any people who helped you secure this donation.

Proliferation of Thank Yous and Perpetuation of the Contact

1. Give Meaningful Recognition to The Funder

The first question you need to ask your donor is what kind of public recognition they prefer. Some will request newspaper articles announcing the grant, others may say that they do not want any form of public recognition. The latter is usually the case with businesses or individuals who wish to protect their name from exposure to many others who may come to them with requests.

Most donors, however, respond very positively to special creative ways the organization chooses to show their appreciation. Unfortunately, funders tell me that very few grantees ever do much in the way of appreciation. It is almost as if those receiving the gifts from private sources are thinking, "They (the funders) have to give the money away to someone." or "They are just doing their jobs. Why should we show them any particular form of recognition?"

If you really want to make an impact, you should ask the question, "What would this organization, or specific individuals in it, really appreciate as recognition?"

Ways to thank the funding organization:

- Newspaper articles or a letter to the editor.
- Articles in your organization's newsletter.
- Informal personal notes, as well as a formal letter.

- Plaque or certificate. (If they have lots of them hanging in their office, it's a good sign they like them!)
- A framed and engraved picture depicting the program they supported. (A theatre group I worked with gave one of these to a major foundation. It was placed in a very prominent spot facing you as you got off the elevator at their office. What a great way to keep *you* on their minds.)
- Awards at your annual meeting or donor reception. (If you know the recipient well, you may want to add some humor to the presentation.)
- Creative, fun gifts. (e.g., a carton of life savers with a note: "Thanks: You are a life saver!!")
- A thank you balloon bouquet delivered to their office.

☐

2. Give Recognition in a Timely Manner

A standard rule of recognition is to give it as soon after the act or the gift as possible. Think for a minute how you feel when you finally get a brief, impersonal thank you note, three months after you have made a contribution to an organization.

As soon as you learn of the donation, you should immediately send the donor an acknowledgment of the gift. You may be planning to do more later, but minimally get out a formal note of appreciation. It is rare that funders receive these,

Proliferation of Thank Yous and Perpetuation of the Contact

so you will be remembered - with fondness!

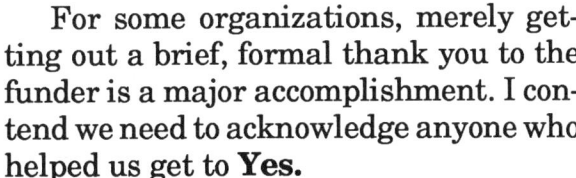

3. Recognize Any People Who Helped You Secure the Donation

For some organizations, merely getting out a brief, formal thank you to the funder is a major accomplishment. I contend we need to acknowledge anyone who helped us get to **Yes**.

Some of the people we need to thank:

- **The individual(s) with whom we worked at the corporation or foundation.** This person was most likely your spokesperson within the corporation or foundation and therefore significantly impacted the **Yes** decision. A personal thank you directed to them is always gratefully received. I would also suggest, for real impact, that you either send their boss a copy of this letter or write a separate letter to their boss indicating how pleasant and efficient (or other appropriate words) their employee was to work with.

- **Any volunteers that spoke on your behalf.** An eloquent, articulate volunteer is worth his/her weight in gold when persuading funders to support our projects. Reward and surprise them with some form of appreciation. They should be one of the first people you invite to your celebration or at least

Getting To Yes In Fund Raising

one of the first to be notified about the grant.

- **Staff members who were involved in developing or writing the proposal.** Part of your celebration should include an acknowledgment of the blood, sweat and tears your staff put into this effort. I usually found that some small creative gift got the biggest response. (Try a wine glass filled with jelly beans, with a note attached, "A toast to a job well done!")

- **People who wrote letters of reference or were used as references.** I have written hundreds of reference letters in support of organizations' funding efforts. <u>One time</u> I received a letter informing me of their grant and thanking me for my supportive letter. I will never hesitate supporting them in the future.

  Remember: You may be needing to ask them for help on some funding request in the future.

- **Executive Director and Board of Directors of the funding body.** On occasions when I have taken the time to acknowledge these folks, I have often received a written response expressing their appreciation for our taking the time to communicate with them. Think of it....if you have ever served on any board of directors, how much of

Proliferation of Thank Yous and Perpetuation of the Contact

your meetings were taken up with reading letters from people expressing their appreciation for your work. Try it, they'll like it! Guaranteed!

☐

The Power in Recognition

I am a firm believer in the incredible power in recognition. When I end my workshops on recognition, I usually share several stories which demonstrate this power.

Our organization was fortunate in connecting with the Hilton when they first came to our community. Wanting to be a good community citizen, they opened their doors to hold 7 major fund raising events. They held our annual Taste of The Valley, an event netting our organization over $35,000. It was obvious that they could not be that generous every year. After hosting these 7 events, they met to determine which two they could sponsor in the ensuing years.

We were fortunately selected. Since I had gotten closely acquainted with the catering manager, I asked her about the criteria they had used to determine whom they would support in the future. Her answer: "Only two organizations gave us any kind of recognition."

When I thought back on what we had done, I recalled that we had sent them numerous notes of appreciation during the course of the planning of the event, we wrote an official letter of appreciation to

---

Dear Hilton Staff,

Thank You!

Thank You!

Thank You!

the Hilton executive staff, we sent a balloon bouquet the day after the event and we presented them with an award at our recognition event. Together it cost us less than $50.00 and took approximately two to three staff hours. Quite an exchange for their facility and staff donation which we valued at $8-$10,000.

My favorite story about the power of recognition was in 1983. I attended a week long management training sponsored by IBM, in response to President Reagan's Private Initiatives Legislation. The week was an incredible experience, personally and professionally. To thank them I wrote one letter to the instructor of the seminar. I decided at the last minute to send copies of that letter to the instructor's boss, the President of IBM, and finally, as a lark, to President Reagan. (One letter, 3 c.c's).

**c.c.
President
Ronald Reagan**

The response from that brief three paragraph letter really brought home the power of recognition. During the ensuing weeks I first received a wonderful note in response from the instructor, thanking me for taking the time to write him (and oh **Yes**, he did notice the c.c.'s). The following week I received an equally nice letter from the instructor's boss (**Yes**, he also remarked on the c.c.'s). The next week the mail man delivered a hand written letter to me from the President of IBM. (I don't know about you, but I would never have even dreamed he would have received it, let alone responded.) Obviously, he doesn't get many letters like this

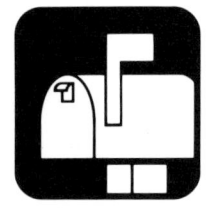

Proliferation of Thank Yous and Perpetuation of the Contact

so he took the time to let me know how much he had appreciated it. He also indicated that it would influence his decision to continue the program. If that's not power in recognition, I don't know what is. Epilogue: You can image that I was haunting the mail box daily, waiting for my letter from Mr. Reagan....Well, I'm still waiting!

Perpetuation of the Contact

One of the significant parts of the fund raising mind-set is the partnership concept. It is, therefore, essential that you see the receipt of a grant as the beginning of an on-going relationship. To perpetuate this, it is important that during the course of your grant, you keep your donors informed of your progress or problems, not just on their evaluation forms but also at your initiative. It is important to keep them on your mailing list and invite them to any special occasions your organization is sponsoring. They cannot always attend, but many funders have shared with me their pleasure in being regularly informed and invited.

Process Evaluation

8 Key Evaluation Questions

It is always important to take some time to assess your fund development process. We most often take this rather simplistic view:

If we get the grant, it is successful. If we don't get the grant, we have failed. In my experience, this may not always be the case.

When we evaluate the process used to obtain a grant, we need to answer the following questions:

1. What were the overall results of our efforts to seek funding in support or initiation of our program?

2. How much paid staff time was involved in securing these funds?

Overall Results

Paid Time

Volunteer Effectiveness

Potential Partnership

Knowledge

Thank Yous

Staff Morale

Future Grants

3. How extensive and effective was our use of volunteers in our fund raising efforts?

4. Have we established a potential partnership with this donor?

5. If we were unsuccessful at obtaining a grant, did we learn anything which will improve our efforts and process in the future?

6. Have we appropriately thanked people who helped us to secure (or attempt to secure) a donation?

7. How is the morale of the staff in the organization, particularly if we did not get to Yes.

8. What can we do in the future to improve our chances of getting grants?

☐

Let's now explore these questions in more depth:.

1. What were the overall results of our efforts to seek funding in support of our program?

If you have set a financial goal, did you achieve it? How many donors turned your proposal down and how many of them supported you? Answering this will give you a sense of how effectively you targeted your efforts. If your ratio of grants received to proposals sent out was very low, you may want to spend more time in the research effort to target potential funders who appear to have a good match with your organization.

Process Evaluation

2. How much paid staff time was involved in securing these funds?

This is one of those painful questions we need to ask after any form of fund raising. After determining the value of that time in dollars, look at the return to the organization in the way of new dollars raised and ask the question, "Was the cost to raise this money too high?" The ideal ratio is approximately 10% costs to raise the money, but this is rarely achieved. It is helpful to aim for a percentage figure for your organization. Then you can evaluate any form of fund raising against that ratio. You may have to experiment with this for awhile. Most organizations tend to discount the enormous amount of time their paid staff puts into fund raising.

3. How effectively did you use volunteers in your fund raising efforts?

This is one of the most important lessons I learned early in fund raising: the key to successful fund raising in an organization is to train and encourage volunteers to be a significant force in most fund raising efforts. Our fund raising had a dramatic upturn when we finally focused on this area. If your paid staff time in fund raising is very high, you will need to focus on delegation skills so as to enable volunteers to support your fund raising efforts. You will also need to institute some training as most volunteers who want to support an organization do not have fund raising skills. (How often we make the mistake of taking any volunteer who hesitantly says, "I'll help with fund raising, if no one else will!")

4. Have we established a potential partnership with this donor?

Often in establishing a partnership, there is a great deal of time and energy expended in the initial phase of establishing the relationship. At first glance it may not appear that your efforts have been worth the gift to your organization. It is important during the evaluation to help your staff and volunteers have a longer view of the value of having established a new partnership. Make plans to nurture this new partner and invite them to be a part of the future work of your organization.

5. If we were unsuccessful at obtaining a grant, did we learn anything which will improve our efforts and process in the future?

As I have previously mentioned, the best way to get good information is to get honest feedback from the funding source that denied your request. The magic question, **"Is there anyway we might get to yes in the future?"** often elicits very useful information as to whether your program, proposal or funding match was the problem with them on this round of funding. This is not the time to be defensive; rather, it is the time to LISTEN and LEARN!

Process Evaluation

6. Have we appropriately thanked people who helped us to secure (or attempt to secure) a donation?

I devoted an entire chapter to this subject because of my strong feelings that this is one of the most powerful ways to get noticed and to increase chances of getting to **Yes** in the future. Just do it and watch the response!

7. How is the morale of the staff in the organization, particularly if our request was denied?

Morale generally suffers in organizations where a rejection is interpreted simply as a failure. Remember, it is important to hold the philosophy that it is only a failure when we have not learned something from the experience. It is also important to provide the necessary training to staff who will be involved in these efforts. Learning by the seat of our pants can have merit only so long.

8. What can we do to better our chances of getting to yes in the future?

As you answer the above questions, you will begin to get a shopping list of ideas on methods you may use to improve your chances in the future. They may include: taking fund raising courses or reading books in the field, consciously developing more potential funding contacts (e.g., join and be active in the chamber of commerce, recruit new board members with those contacts, attend workshops and meetings where you know funders will be presenting or attending), hiring a consultant to teach or motivate the organization in issues of fund raising or to <u>review</u> your proposals, etc.

☐

PIE Method of Evaluation

In response to your evaluation sessions, you may want to think of the word PIE. Your recommendations for future fund raising efforts will most likely fall into these three categories:

P -Preserve

I -Improve

E -Eliminate

If we don't occasionally slow down and evaluate our efforts, we may be missing an opportunity, as Marlene Wilson, noted volunteer trainer and author says, "to learn from our mistakes and well-dones." This is particularly helpful when you are just beginning your efforts to seek private funds for your organization.

☐

Concluding Comments:

More and more organizations are competing for these scarce private funds. Those agencies that learn from their experience and make adjustments and plans for improvement are greatly enhancing their chances of <u>Getting To Yes In Fund Raising.</u>

☐

Personal Tidbits
(some new, some review)

1. The mind-set you carry with you regarding fund raising can be your greatest asset or your biggest detraction.
2. When seeking donations, refer to your clients', not your agency's needs. Remember: Donors give us money for our clients!
3. Fund raising is 90% preparation and planning.
4. You are most often successful in fund raising when you have an excellent program AND superb communication skills to convince others to say **Yes** to your cause.
5. Know as much as you can about a funder before directly approaching them.
6. Patience and persistence are two virtues a fund raiser must have.
7. Recognition of your funders (and all who supported your efforts) is a powerful, frequently underused tool which can enhance your future success in fund raising.
8. People give to people, not to causes or organizations.
9. Be visible in arenas where there might be funders present.
10. Use volunteers and clients to state your case whenever possible.
11. Funders give when there is a mutual interest established. (Always ask: What's in it for them?)
12. You can work as hard for $50.00 as you can for $50,000. Learn to distinguish between them.
13. You cannot attract funds for your organization when its credibility is not intact.

14. Your best sources of funding are your current or previous sources.
15. Develop an attractive prospectus and update it annually.
16. Learn from your "No, but good luck in the future" experiences.
17. Always Celebrate Your Successes!
18. If you can succinctly and enthusiastically articulate a real need in your community, there is a funder out there for you.
19. Remember when things seem pretty grim: Babe Ruth struck out 1,130 times in his career!
20. Hang on to your dream! Without it, you may give up before **Getting to Yes in Fund Raising.**

Getting To Yes in Fund Raising

Parting Thoughts

With the exception of professionals in the field of fund raising, most people enter the world of fund development as I did: believing in a cause or a vision and eventually discovering that to bring it into reality would mean the raising of substantial funds.

Learning this art of fund raising took me many years of trial and error, stop and start, disappointment and elation. Sometimes when I was in the midst of doing it every day, I wondered if it was all worthwhile. Looking back now, I know it was.

I hope that this book has given you the inspiration to try, the tools to aid in the process, and perhaps a few tips and secrets to assist you in your journey to

Getting to Yes In Fund Raising.

Appendix

Worksheet for Fund Raising

1. What problem are we trying to solve?

2. What are some objectives of that program, project? How will we know that we have succeeded?

3. What resources are needed from business/foundation/individuals to assist us in this project, program?

4. What foundations/corporations/individuals might we approach for support and what is our connection with them? (e.g., common interest in the problem, personal contact, etc.)

5. What might we include in an attractive agency prospectus?

6. Who will prepare the case statement or write the proposal?

7. What are the elements of strategy for our oral presentation? (i.e., Who will present the case? What do I bring to "Show & Tell"? What's in it for the funder to give to us? How do I convince them of our need, our ability, leadership, return on investment? In other words, How will I get to **Yes**?)

8. If needed, how will we keep this program going in the future?

9. What are meaningful and creative ways to show appreciation to our funders?

True Dollar Value of Volunteers — Worksheet*

Volunteer Job Title: _____

1. Equivalent Salaried Job Classification
   (Based on a comparison of the tasks and responsibilities described in the volunteer job description with those of an equivalent employee)
   Equivalent Salaried Job Title: _____
2. Annual Salary for Equivalent Salaried Classif. $ _____
3. Value of Benefits Package:
   FICA .... $ _____
   Health Insurance .... $ _____
   Life Insurance .... $ _____
   Workers Compensation Insurance ......$ _____
   Retirement .... $ _____
   Other Benefits: .... $ _____
           Total Value of Benefits: $ _____

4. Annual Salary + Benefits Package = ... $ _____
5. Established Annual Work Hours for
   Agency: _____ hours/week x 52 weeks = _____ Hrs.
6. Hours Paid but Not Worked Annually:
   Annual Leave .... _____ Hrs.
   Paid Holidays .... _____
   Paid Sick Leave .... _____
   Total Hours Paid/not worked: .... _____
7. Established Annual Hours
       Hours Paid but not worked =
       ACTUAL WORK HOURS ANNUALLY: .... _____
8. Total Annual Compensation Package
       Actual Work Hours Annually = ... _____
   True Dollar Value of Each Hour of Volunteer
   Time in This Job Description: .... $ _____

*Source: By Neil Karn, "Money Talks: A Guide to Establishing the True Dollar Value of Volunteer Time," The Journal of Volunteer Administration, Winter (1982-83), pp. 1-7.

Bibliography

Flanagan, Joan. The Grassroots Fundraising Book. Contemporary Books, Inc., Chicago, 1982.

Klein, Kim. Grassroots Fundraising Videotapes. The Youth Project, 2335 18th Street N.W., Washington, D.C. 20009.

Lord, James Gregory. The Raising of Money. Third Sector Press, Cleveland.

Scribner, Susan M. How to Ask For Money Without Fainting. Scribner and Associates, 1990.

Vineyard, Sue. Marketing Magic For Volunteer Programs. Heritage Arts Publishing, Downers Grove, Illinois, 1984.

Ziglar, Zig. Secrets of Closing The Sale. Berkley Books, New York, 1984.

About the Author

Betty Stallings, MSW, is a national trainer, consultant, author and keynote speaker on fund raising, volunteerism, leadership and change. A native of Philadelphia, Pennsylvania, she earned a B.S. Degree at Ohio Wesleyan University and an MSW at The University of Wisconsin.

Formerly, Betty was the Founder and 13 year Executive Director of Pleasanton, California's Valley Volunteer Center, considered one of the nation's most effective, creative centers. While at the Center she initiated numerous programs which have served as national models of volunteer utilization. Besides her professional work in the fields of fund raising and volunteerism, Betty volunteers for numerous health, educational and community activities and has received many citations and awards for these endeavors.

Seeking resources for nonprofit organizations became Betty's hallmark. While at the Volunteer Center she obtained hundreds of grants from major foundations and corporations, initiated successful signature fund raising events and raised financial and in-kind resources from individuals and small businesses in the community, totalling in the millions of dollars.

In response to the many people who began asking Betty for her "secrets" to successful fund raising, she began to present workshops around the U.S. and Canada. With the continued encouragement of many workshop participants, she has now shared her tips in **Getting To Yes In Fund Raising**.

Betty's rich background in fund raising and volunteer management, her broad-based experience as a volunteer and her humor, vitality and inspiration have made her a sought after trainer and speaker.

For information on workshops or lectures, Betty can be contacted at Stallings & Associates, 1717 Courtney Avenue, Suite 201, Pleasanton, California, 94588 or call/FAX (415) 426-8335.